A Place to Stand

A Place to Stand

Mike Fisher

This book or any portion thereof may not be reproduced or used in any manner whatsoever without the express written permission of the copyright holder except for the use of brief quotations in a book review.

The right of Mike Fisher to be identified as the author of this work has been asserted by him in accordance with the Copyright, Design and Patents Act 1988.

First Printing, 2025

Published by Clayhanger Press
.
7 Highfield Court
Newcastle under Lyme
Staffordshire
ST5 3LT

www.clayhangerpress.co.uk

All rights reserved.

ISBN-13: 978-1-917017-11-4

For friends and family
In the hope that these
Poems will be enjoyed
And live beyond me
On a shelf somewhere

February 2025

Contents

"GIVE ME A PLACE TO STAND AND I WILL MOVE THE WORLD"	8
MIND BODY PROBLEM 1	9
A CHANCE MEETING	10
OUR WALK BY TREES	11
PRINT PAINT AND PETALS	12
A RIFF ON SOLITUDE	13
ATLANTIC CHALLENGE	14
OCEAN DEITY	15
THE YACHT JUNO	16
A HORSE CALLED BARBARY CARRIES RICHARD II	17
TURF ACCOUNT	18
THE GATOR MAN	19
ANAXIMENES' PARADOX	20
THE GOOD LIFE	21
PHILOSOPHY IN A TIME OF COVID	22
WHEN LOSS GOES VIRAL	23
PITUITARY HORMONES ARE IN CHARGE	24
OUT OF THE YELLOW HOUSE	25
MIND BODY PROBLEM II	26
TWENTY YEARS AFTER - A PLAN COMES TOGETHER	27
VALENTINE	28
HOW LONG IS A KISS?	29
BREAKFAST IN THE GARDEN	30
SO SORRY	31
FAITH AND TRUST	32
TODAY THE LIFE OF BEES	33
SUPERPOSITION	34

HUBBLE'S HEAVEN	35
A TRINITY OF FORMS,	36
APPROACHING ANGLESEY AT DUSK	37
NOVEMBER WOODS	38
THE DISUSED RAILWAY TRACT AT OAKAMOOR	39
BAMBURGH BEACH	40
ST CUTHBERT	41
LIFELONG THESPIANS	42
MESSAGES ARRIVE AT BAMBURGH CASTLE	43
ALL THIS I REMEMBER	44
THE LUNACY OF MEDICINE	45
THE WARD ROUND CIRCA 1965	46
THE CLINICO-PSYCHO-SOCIAL MODEL OF CARE BECOMES THE	47
CLINICO-PATHOLOGICAL MODEL	47
WOLSTANTON DEEP PIT	48
THE QUARRY	49
SHROPSHIRE SPRING	50
THE BOARS HEAD	51
ITERATION	52
HERACLITUS YOU ARE MISTAKEN	53
WATER AND EARTH FIRE AND AIR	54
THE UNIVERSE LISTENS TO THE POETS	55
BEGINNING AND END – TWO SIDES OF THE SAME COIN	56

"Give me a place to stand and I will move the world"

Archimedes first, then JFK at Camelot
My father too would use the phrase
That captures a philosophy
Through which to lever life

A tolerant man until a line was crossed.
Strong principles, it was his way
Old fashioned out of fashion
Heels dug in he held his ground

So few material goods to mark a life
Some trinkets and a walking stick.
The greater gift was wisdom
Passed from father to his son

He knew the ground on which he stood
From there he changed my world

Mind Body Problem 1

Slippers scuff scullery tiles
Feet shuffle no longer lifted
Shoulders rounded stooped
Jowls loose
Skin paper thin

Within the grey cells
Amaranthine memories
Summoned at will
Vivid awkward risqué
      Transcend decay

A Chance Meeting

Woodland warmed by winter sun
signals an awaking
branches stretch as yet unclothed
          buds but a promise of the canopy to come
underfoot potholed and puddled
the path slips beneath boots
gone the firm track of last summer
      ahead four figures focus into family
      my son's son runs arms outstretched
            springs hugs renews

Our walk by trees

Close to the old gates we left the car
Along the path across the river grubby and slow
Passed the church and through the kissing gate

Near to the wood we climbed the style
The trees had shed their leaves, now trampled underfoot.
Ahead the fence was breached, the wire mesh bent right back
On hands and knee we scrambled through, first you then me
Surprised! we laughed and squeezed each other's hand

Along the path, we hoped to see the deer, none came
Steep between the trees we reached the ridge
Less short of breath than we expected for our years
Seven ancient beeches trunks misshapen gnarled
Alive before our birth they'll oversee our passing

Mature trees left behind we wandered on
Searched out the newly planted saplings
Labelled Charlie, Will and Christopher
Sound roots now set to grow, branch out and soar
Growth we will see for all too short a time.

Few other walkers to intrude, disturb a closeness,
Memories joys and sorrows shared
Retrace our steps back to the waiting car

Print paint and petals

A Gallery print bought years ago.
Vincent's Sunflowers
Not the famous one, all yellows and impasto,
But painted four days earlier
To welcome Gauguin to the house at Arles

It moved through student rooms, until transformed
Over painted by a girlfriend
Sunflowers risen radiant
Brush strokes real recall the love
The joy excitement Vincent felt
Glorious still – it hangs within my gaze.

Adjacent on a table
Sunflowers bought two days ago
for two pounds fifty
Slowly sag

A Riff on Solitude

Most companionable companion
solitude
apart not lonely
a choice not imposed

Sacred contemplation
seeking sublimation insight peace
a passion and a gallantry
a nun's hermitage solitude its aim

Solitude a cell
the penitent prisoner
meditates alone
a punishment and privilege
of freedom friendship forests and moors

Alone with birdsong
whispering leaves and sunlight
nature's solitude
offers tranquil sylvian bliss
a passion and courageousness

Today mindfulness
Commercialized and loud
Solitude nowhere

Atlantic Challenge

'Skipper, on deck!' 'The kite's blown!'
Shredded, the spinnaker's
Torn remnants shoved through the letterbox
'Now hoist the number three'
Within minutes calm, the winds divide
The main sail flaps limp
'hold steady or we gybe'

Thai curry in a yellow bowl,
Mid-Atlantic take away
Passed hand to hand along the cockpit
Comes with spoon
Replete and satisfied, the empty bowls passed back
Galley sink on gimbles lists at forty-five degrees
Tests washers, wipers expertise

Horta beckons, three days out
The rain comes down as
Water drips from off the helmsman's nose
Unexpected, music fills the boat and deck
And lifts the mood maintains morale
Then thoughts of Peter's bar and solid land
Intersect with concentration on the task to hand

Ocean Deity

Move gently across my surface
Show respect, stand in awe
Sextant, watch, chart and rule
'Ocean Master' you may become
But wind and waves are mine
My white mares prance
Yet in a moment rear up
Unseating the unwary

Today fair passage
Home port in days
Atlantic Challenge, you've called it
But in truth Atlantic homage

The Yacht Juno

Ahead, dolphins race the bow wave
Leaping, encouraging sleek
Smaller than those at Disney
They disappear as they came
No compass, no cares

Tuna, fresh from a can
Spread between bread that's ten days old
Moistened with mayonnaise.
Lunch over, dirty plates and knives,
Greasy in the galley

On the foredeck, sails hang loose
Crew hushed, the silence
Broken only by soft sounds
As surf laps on the lea
The mast creaks.

Thoughts turn to home, a week distant
Disagreements, tensions set aside
              Swept overboard
Sails and moods trimmed
Home port our shared ambition

A Horse Called Barbary Carries Richard II

Proud to be doing God's work
least carrying one who does
he's anointed, me just chosen
but I look the part, groomed to perfection
him too, except today
bare headed
dust scattered on his scalp
crowds jeering

Apparently God withdrew his blessing
gave it someone else
pity, I liked Richard
gone to the tower they say
Monarchy, permanence
it's me provides stability
'Long Live the Roan'

War pestilence assassins
Kings they come and go
well graced actors who leave the stage

The new man, arrogant
no grip in his knees spurs turned in
I'll carry him to his deathbed in
France then back here to the Abbey

Turf Account

An each-way bet
Not based on form
Simply the name,
'Pascals Wager'

An older horse, reluctant
turns towards the tape
Fences higher than expected
appear through autumn mist
the going soft, hooves sink in
fetlocks stiff sore
A stumble,
Neck is lifted nostrils flared
Ahead
a Grail shaped cup
or just a grave

the final bend, a camera flash....

The Gator Man

Joe parks his truck
enters the cage around
the swimming pool
eyes the extant dinosaur
that thinks
the pool was built for him

Wetlands drained
concrete spread
tennis courts, a garage for three cars
the gators' kingdom lost
usurped by
single story homes

A wire lasso then cloths thrown over eyes
Joe leaps - sits on the armour-plated head
wraps gaffer tape around the jaws
Made safe transported
to a reservation far away
that or maybe shot

Anaximenes' Paradox

Open mouthed I breathe onto your lips
as I have these years
warm moist air
a caress from me to you

Of late your memory lost
new ways not seen before
anger aggression

lips pursed tight I sigh
the air is cool on your forehead
you startle recoil

The Good Life

Ugly argumentative, Socrates
sought the recipe for a good life
virtue wisdom knowledge purpose
embracing truth overcoming strife

Aristotle's Phaedrus
set down much more
act justly and live life devoid of fear
think clearly create Eudaimonia

unexamined our life can never be
faithful, the good life we strive to see
pursue the nature of reality
add to the good life recipe

Philosophy in a time of Covid

Jeremy Bentham, still extant
Not underground like Immanuel Kant

Stares at us from his glass fronted case
Utilitarian thoughts, for us to embrace

Body preserved and philosophy too
Ideas from which a health service grew

Pain and pleasure his two extremes
Measured by new found calculus

The greatest good for the greatest number
No thoughts of your own just knuckle under

Lock yourself down, stay in your home
Follow the science all alone

When loss goes viral

waving through windows, touch denied
separation, love at a distance
misunderstanding mix-up misconstruction
fear causes us to duck and dodge,
the price of safety, isolation loss
of friendships family love
alarm least the virus creeps
unnoticed through walls measured
in microns, yet a nuclear threat
that's supercharged
a boorish guest spoiling the party
as variations come and go
jumps ill-mannered host to host
smooth as butter spread on toast
slips down throat to suffocate

The plague has passed
perspective gained
amor vincet omnia

Pituitary Hormones are in charge

Nestled in the Turkish saddle,
Born from neural tracts
Hormone couriers tell the organs
How and when to act

Summoning deeds, irrational mood
They cycle as the moon
Nocturnal trough, then magnitude
The carbon chains commune,

A goitre throat, the cretin brain
Our growth against a chart
Adrenaline that hides the pain
Beyond our will or personal art

To tame these Herculean chains
Replace the havoc, peace regain
Assert control and seize the reins
Needs drugs to dull the pain

Out of the Yellow House

Damaged temporal lobe moods swing
Fingers twitch as if to pick
Imagined insects by their wings
Lips smack, jaw chews, a lunatic
Locked away by Dr Felix Rey
Fastened in a padded room

Infirmity both midwife and destroyer
Of the art that captured light
Sunflowers cornfields starry night
Carved on canvas with a palette knife
Visionary insight tortured life
Vincent felt the rush the joy then left

Mind Body Problem II

Nails distort, keratin laid down in ridges
Elastin gone skin thins bruises tears
Memory thinks it knows best
But may play false misplacing 'stuff'

Hair thins, grows slowly or maybe quicker
Chalk replaces bone, becomes both
Brittle and soft collapsing under
The stresses and strains of aged joints

Eyesight clouds, cataract closes the curtain
What remains is vivid
Cinemascope and technicolour images
Conjured out of memory from weary grey matter

There detail vibrant hues on full canvas
Often bright and impasto oils full of emotion
At times soft water colours hint at
Softer moods, enchantments of love

Twenty years after - A plan comes together

At last! Amsterdam
canals to cruise bike and tram girls in windows
churches and candlewax
aching backs

Art is what we came to see, a madman but we stand in awe
trace his life, through …. London Paris Arles
starry night and sunflowers
wooden bed and wheatfield crows

We walk the sunny side of the canal,
baroque houses close to Dam Square
dark discreet loud bars, cafés,
unsmiling men smoke acrid cigarettes

Café Tertula, family run was further than we thought
out the door a queue two generations younger than we

I take a childish chocolate cake
labelled 'beginner' so buy a 'regular' as well

consumed, walk back along the shaded side
perception unaltered, packet brownies perhaps?

at supper a wide seraphic grin conversation slow
you hold my hand support my wavy gait

Valentine

In a foreign tongue I count the petals of a daisy
Je t'aime, un peu, beaucoup,
passionnement, a la folie
Simultaneously reciting Latin verbs,
Amo, amas, amat, amamas…
Memories burnt into my mind, always there
Infinite as the universe – love has no ending.

How long is a kiss?

Thirteen point eight billion years? – a multiverse?
Is that less than infinity? but which infinity do you speak of?

Lips dissolve time and space are one,
Morphing, star, red giant then white dwarf

Never to end locked by the sculptor
two souls kiss embrace

Salt taste on canvas, Venus happens from a shell,
'will China and Africa meet?' 'love has no ending'

'time passes' Llareggub, year after year unaltered
a place in quantum time for passion, love

Never taken, kisses given Poly Garter dreams of babies
Clocks fail to move. How long is a kiss?

Breakfast in the garden

Early morning sun
Calm, no earnest chatter from the radio
Sourdough two days old,
Toasted and revived
With honey from a friend

Gentle musing, in my head plans unfold
Odd how structured yet unheard
Is the conversation.
'A circuit of the lake? Perhaps some weeding?'
That suggestion quickly set aside!

The days agenda fixed, more honey
      heather honey, delicious

So sorry

Berries, slide
from stalks
soft between
thumb and finger

Warmed by sun
dissolving on
my tongue
wonderfully sweet

Those picked
to carry home
to you
all eaten

Faith and Trust

Early morning and the rain is close,
In the forecast, an almighty storm.
The warmth of bed still clings
Pyjamas rumpled, slippers worn,
He moves downstairs and
Out the kitchen door,
The time is now

Bought in expectation of the rain
He scatters grass-seed, to revive
renew bare patches in the lawn
Instructions call for preparation,
Scarify, top dressing, rake well in
At almost eighty, there's no time,
The rain is near.

Today the Life of Bees

Today we have the history of bees. Yesterday
we had quadratic equations and tomorrow morning
we will have the problem of climate change, but today
today we have the history of bees. In the school's
flower garden white hives give home and shelter

You will sketch the bee's back leg; corbiculae which
fill with pollen that is latter spread as they flit flower
to flower suck nectar from sweet nasturtiums
Draw the hive the landing stage, air traffic control where
bees arrive regular as the manifest

Describe the waggle dance where polarized sunlight's
used to map both distance and direction
workers colleagues all can read the signs
sophisticated language of the bees -a dance
geometry to draw in workbooks

Explain why six is strong. The waxy cells hexagonal
capacious optimal in shape contain the honey
that we spread on golden toast or eat from off a spoon
What engineers these bees to build a comb within
the hive within a school flower garden

Be aware – this story is of sex and passion
a double helix splits, then different gametes
recombine Drone and Queen the act of procreation
surprised, embarrassed you may blush. Next term
we'll cover this in human physiology

Hooded and disguised you will become an apiarist
as such steal hard-won winter food cause bees to swarm
record this stage and how a hive reborn renewed
brings sweetness and life's cycle goes another round
Today we have the history of bees

Superposition

Apollo's shadow marks the dial,
The seasons cycle, tides return unchanged.
We sense, a never-ending flow.
Wisdom passed from father to the son
Runs through generations,
ends where it began.

Recollected memories, still as clear
No different now from then,
dissolve time,
which ceases to exist.
The archer, bow drawn both to future and the past
let's fly times' arrow, unexpected, it does not move.

So time and space are one.
Symbols on a page, predicting entropy.
Quantum tells an end to time.
Defying comprehension,
Particles at once both here
and there.

Hubble's Heaven

Gravitational waves, dust squeezed
unseen muons, quarks, divine Higgs bosun
singularities and galaxies
multihued the pillars of creation

On earth 'The word made flesh'
supplications rise, float free
compline, vespers, prayers ascend
'above the bright blue sky'

Quantum and Deity, Entanglement and faith
ineffable, exciting, insoluble as Schrodinger's cat
await a still small voice 'Major Tom to ground control'.

A Trinity of Forms,

lacey on the branch but
underfoot ice fells the unwary
crystal stars drift into snowmen
icebergs crumble
cascading onto the deck
ninety pence a bag

driving generators
steam scalds
sings from a kettle
fog on the breath
obscures reflected images
cools on the face glass

tumbling from rocky heights
springs and waterfalls
disappear into a misty haze
return as drizzle
membranes rupture
soaking sheets

Approaching Anglesey at Dusk

Ablaze with silent light
suspended, straits beneath
bridging worlds

scriptoria to the east
standing stones
and barrows on the isle

a castle building king invades
arrogance presumption
language supressed

impervious to pike and canon
beliefs traditions
competence passed
father to son to grandson

stories and poetry
folklore and custom
relevant as the calculus

November Woods

Leaves of ancient oaks hold fast while
those from hazel beech and ash drift down
create anew the earth

Years past I kicked the fallen leaves, heard
rustle crackle crunch, marvelled at
the coloured quilt beneath my feet

Eight score years are gone
steps slow, balance unsure
I take the path most trodden

November sun dips
low almost out of sight, air chills
another year is through

The Disused Railway Tract at Oakamoor

Trodden underfoot by boots and
wheels of centuries gone
origin and terminus holdfast
defying time

track and rails are lost
as is the copper ore they bore,
train and trucks no longer back and forth with rocks
and crocks and ware from bottle kilns

like a mouldy multi-layered cake
sandstone cliffs green with moss
shade the southern side
recall time past whilst
tall larch telegraph the future

use and purpose constantly renewed
today a thrush sings for a mate
off lead dogs, chase slimy tennis balls
tiny kids scrunch fallen leaves in
wellington boots red, yellow green signal
re-creation family fun

Bamburgh Beach

Long shadows stretch
       towards the approaching tide
An autumn sun hangs low
       spills soft and golden light
across the sand,

Waves break, then gently
spread along the shore.
The ocean, cold across my toes
       delights and thrills as much
       At seventy as it did at six

St Cuthbert

We stride across bladderwrack,
ridges in sand regular as a ploughed field
recall receding waves, expose foreshore,
mudflats, sands which stretch
too far for us to see the returning tide

we claim the beach as ours,
then unexpected, a seal
eyes pecked out, open belly wound
dumped carelessly by currents,
tides from Holy Lindisfarne

sacked by Vikings laid to waste
the ancient monastery abandoned,
carefully the fleeing monks
lift Cuthbert's coffin, carry
it across the causeway

over dunes to Durham there
a cathedral crypt in which
the body finds a resting place
remembered and revered
the hallowed saint's remains do not decay

Lifelong Thespians

I walk the beach, above is Bamburgh Castle
Sometime home to mighty Harry Hotspur
Thoughts drift back to when some three score years ago
Ankles hidden by a royal blue frock
I crossed the stage to take my Harry's hand
"Kate come, thou art perfect in lying down"
The bawd of Avon causes us to smirk
"Go to you giddy goose" my set response
Rich are the treasures memory unearths
Nectar on the tongue a sweet remembrance
Until forgetfulness erases joy
Today the sands of time run in reverse
Then we were players on a smaller stage
We had our entrance now too soon it ends

Messages arrive at Bamburgh Castle

Within these battlements
Men fought and died
A bloody physical fight
Opponents, face to face.

Today two messages - a brother, then a friend
Pressed to a fight they did not seek.
The foe broke through unseen
And took possession, killing both.

Alone, no family near
The ventilator switched to stop.
Plastic figures, Lego like
Move into place a sterile bag

Discharged to die at home;
Refusing drink, her mind made up
face turned towards the wall
the time has come to slip away.

No swords, no arrows flew and yet,
A brother and a friend are dead.
Lives measured, not by valour
But the good they brought
The love they showered on those they knew

All this I Remember

Blue marks on shoulders and on arms
were outward signs the miners had inhaled
the dust which settled in their lung,
a noxious dust, from both the coal and stone
foretold a suffocating death,
pitiful pension paid to wives
this I remember

The Blythe Bridge factory men
had ulcers in their nose
from fumes of chromium used
to plate the shiny kettles, pots and pans.
Cancer brought on workers who
risked all to hold their job.
this I remember

Five miles away, a factory set in countryside,
Cups, casseroles and china plates,
were decorated with lead paint which,
carried on the brushes and the lips of paintresses
destroyed the red blood cells.
Pale workers cast aside.
this too I remember

The Lunacy of Medicine

1900

Leather straps and iron padlock
Bind the lunatic
Inhumanity to madness,
Brutalise both him and me.

1968

A secure padded cell
The patient grins across at me
Shut in together

2020

Medication, now supreme
Hidden from our view
Binds the sufferer, makes him prisoner,
Just as rooms and padlocks do.

The Ward Round Circa 1965

Cast iron beds in ordered rows
laundered apron, pleated cap
sister's authority clearly shows
green badged students white starched coats
pockets bulge with stethoscopes
'Bedside Diagnosis' a dogeared crib

A patient is pressed to join the play
sheet and blankets stripped away
to help the 'dresser' perform their best
God-like consultants teach through discord
happy to humiliate feelings ignored
time for ignorance to be explored

Grouped round a bed, eyes downcast
trying to hide to be bypassed
No! step forward you're selected
embarrassed and clumsy the student struggles
to hear the rhonchi the rales and the bubbles
but all this effort is brought to naught
comedy for the teacher - tragedy for the taught

The Clinico-psycho-social Model of Care becomes the Clinico-pathological Model

Physicians taught befriended treated listened touched and reassured
Helped distressed and broken people live with sickness and their pain

A scalpel taken to the model
Psychosocial's been excised
No more illness just disease
Codes in books and mortuaries
Physicians now must follow pathways
'Patient centred' is revised

Treat the tests and not the person, swabs and x-rays, scans and scopes
Latest and best, shiny and grand, new technologies are to hand

Lists created; patients wait marking time on sallow corpses
of the ones who 'sadly died', never now to reach the top

Hiding on the wards accountants,
managers who count the cash,
must avoid financial crash

Tidier without the illness easier now that socials gone
A new and costed/broken system

Wolstanton Deep Pit

Summoned from the surgery breathless
don a boiler suit brilliant white, identifies
in the gloom below

Built for trucks not men, the cage
jolts clatters down a thousand feet
waiting train slow noisy, ten minutes to the face

Crushed misshapen leg
trousers bloodied torn the bone protrudes
one ankle tied against the other

Morlock mates, anxious concerned
'cost do owt?'
two grains of morphine ampule, needle, arm

Time slows – train dawdles, track uneven
Cecil whimpers curses, then shaft-bottom
the hoist a waiting ambulance

The Quarry

Form IV, we learnt of millstone grit
And sandstone heaved from out the sea.
Today pebbles smoothed by passing feet, tumble the unwary

Birch and stunted oaks enfold the slopes
And yellow flowers of gorse,
Proclaim a time for kissing, always here

In heather undergrowth, a pheasant hides
Above a buzzard circles and below
The sparrows hop from twig to rock to shrub

A laceration in the hillside, memories
When my son climbed up the quarry side
Ignoring risk, adventure uppermost

Today, he fears for me,
The virus crown shapes social isolation.
More distance than these forty years

Shropshire Spring

Gold dust spreads across the seat
And will not brush away
Pollen falls from hazel catkins
Out the hedge row cut this day

Home from sister's Shropshire farm
The tall, tailed twigs, attest
To air that's fresh a day that's free
Spent muddy, mindful and unstressed

High on cluttered mantel shelf
The vase has sat some days
When leaves appear a spring-time green
Though half expected still amaze.

The Boars Head

When Phoebus shines on the inn
And baskets hang from the wall
Dahlia fuchsia petunia filled
A sundial vertical over the door
Never forces time

The hostelry sign hangs free
Many a year since Boars roamed here
gone the forest the pond remains
Moorhen unconcerned

Sky is attached to the chimney
A yellow box 'Heart Start' magic
Ivy covers bricks but
Gives the lie to 'founded 1893'
The beer is good

The hostelry sign hangs free
Many a year since Boars roamed here
gone the forest the pond remains
Claw foot Moorhen unconcerned

Iteration

Relearning truths from generations gone
Sagacity bequeathed by ancestors
Wisdom enlightenment chicken and egg

No cosmic clocks to measure out a life
I am both newborn and Methuselah
Relearning truths from generations gone

Born of stardust there return again
To weaved anew refresh the universe
Wisdom enlightenment chicken and egg

Fading to nearly nothing - entropy
Inflation causes me to rise again
Relearning truths from generations gone

My destination is my origin
Both genesis and termination
Wisdom enlightenment chicken and egg

Truths learning knowledge all return and then
It is our understanding sets us free
Relearning truths from generations gone
Wisdom enlightenment chicken and egg

Heraclitus You Are Mistaken

Today is not a day for hesitance
the sky a blue silk scarf float's
on banks of yellow gorse that
signal 'kissing an eternal joy'

the dusty path, the bridge
our padlock clipped to a rusting mesh
cool remembered water tickles toes
unchanged we step into its flow

Today is not a day for philosophers
time can stand still, eighteen just
as we were twice twenty years ago
Alive, in love, fearless

Water and Earth Fire and Air

imbalance, off balance, excess deficiency
sanguine phlegmatic melancholy rage

rules of four ancient law
seek to explain happiness and pain

black bile and winter, cold and remote
yellow bile summer, ambitious cutthroat

red and black, yellow and green
anger and sadness mind and spleen

Aristotle Plato Galen Empedocles
physicians today grey, humourless

The Universe Listens to the Poets

Dusty rose leaves in a bowl
the bird both sang and spoke
foretold my four score years – now nearly spent

measured on an Apple watch
the working week the joy of Sunday lunch
sun and sands a two-week summer break
these days are where I spend my life

an archer, bow drawn both
to future and the past
let's fly times' arrow

unexpected it does not move,
quantum equations have no need of 't' merely
entropy requires that delta S is
always greater than or equals zero

walk up the mountain path
time quickens, in the valley friends age less
their clocks run slow

        listen time passes

Beginning and End – Two sides of the same coin

My father said that death is part of life
Though life must end, still nothing is destroyed.
Our atoms scattered through the universe
Indestructible they're redeployed
The second law says so; they are preserved,
Particles arrive, then leave us for the stars
Exuberant energy, quantum thrust
To unknown bourns in which we have to trust
Perchance to dream of immortality?
A state as yet we cannot comprehend
Hid both by physics and a deity
Aside from faith, these questions have no end.
This Earthly life we know is unsurpassed
Heaven here; held loosely in our grasp

Cover Design by Clayhanger Press
from a photograph by Mike Fisher

Typesetting by Roger Bloor

www.clayhangerpress.co.uk

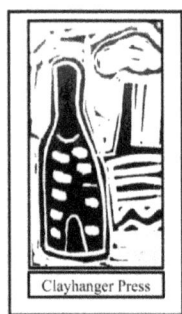

www.ingramcontent.com/pod-product-compliance
Lightning Source LLC
Chambersburg PA
CBHW041307240426
43661CB00037B/1459/J